LLOYD GEORGE AND THE FIRST WORLD WAR

Stewart Ross

Illustrated by Martin Salisbury

Wayland

LIFE AND TIMES

Adviser: Dr Maguire of the Department
of Humanities, Brighton Polytechnic, East Sussex
Editor: E.J. Clark
First published in 1987 by Wayland (Publishers) Ltd
61 Western Road, Hove, East Sussex BN3 1JD, England
© Copyright 1987 Wayland (Publishers) Ltd
British Library Cataloguing in Publication Data
Ross, Stewart
Lloyd George and the First World War. —
(Life and times)
1. World War, 1914–1918—Juvenile literature
I. Title II. Salisbury, Martin III. Series
940.3   D522.7
ISBN 1–85210–241–1
Phototypeset by DP Press, Sevenoaks, Kent
Printed in Italy by G. Canale & C.S.p.A, Turin
Bound in Great Britain at the Bath Press, Avon

Contents

1 DAVID LLOYD GEORGE

The young Liberal

Between the years 1906 and 1922 David Lloyd George was the most exciting figure in British politics. His ideas shaped the country's future, his speeches thrilled all who heard them and, as Prime Minister, he guided the nation firmly through the most horrific war it had ever faced. Yet this great man came from very humble origins.

When David was only one year old his father died, leaving his wife and children in great poverty. The family moved from Manchester to Wales, where they were looked after by David's uncle Richard. The young David was clearly a brilliant child and when he left school the family made sacrifices to have him trained as a solicitor.

After qualifying in 1884, David was a great success in the courts, earning a good reputation as a lawyer. Before long his love of oratory and debate attracted him to politics. In 1890 he was elected a Liberal MP for Caernarvon Boroughs, in North Wales, and he quickly made a name for himself as an up-and-coming young radical.

In his early years in Parliament David bravely opposed the Anglo-Boer war of 1899–1902. He also supported Welsh nationalism, particularly against the privileged position of Church of England schools in Wales. Therefore, when the Liberals won the 1905 general election, the 'Welsh Wizard', as he had now come to be known, was an obvious choice as a government minister.

Above *David Lloyd George when he first entered Parliament in 1890. The young politician soon made a name for himself with his fiery speeches.*

Left *Growing up in North Wales David learned quickly, listening eagerly to the stories and opinions of the adults around him.*

Chancellor

In 1905, at the age of forty-two, Lloyd George was appointed to the post of President of the Board of Trade in the Liberal cabinet. The young minister set about his task with customary energy. He introduced laws to improve the living conditions of sailors, to protect the rights of inventors, and to reorganize the port of London.

In 1908 Lloyd George moved to the much more important position of Chancellor of the Exchequer. His first budget, the 'People's Budget,' so angered the mainly Conservative House of Lords that they rejected it – something that had not been done for hundreds of years, and which broke an unwritten law, that the Lords did not interfere with finance bills.

As Chancellor of the Exchequer, Lloyd George introduced state sickness and unemployment pay, which could be collected from the Post Office.

As a result, much of the Lords' power to interfere with the wishes of the House of Commons was permanently removed. Later, in 1911, 'The people's David' introduced the remarkable National Insurance Act, which for the first time gave some workers sickness and unemployment pay, a measure which is regarded as one of the great achievements of Liberalism.

Since the early twentieth century, relations between Britain and Germany had become increasingly strained. War finally broke out in August, 1914. By 1916 it was clear that the leadership of the Liberal Prime Minister, Henry Asquith, was unsatisfactory. Lloyd George had already made a great contribution to Britain's war effort as Minister of Munitions. Now, with the support of the Conservatives, he found himself in the highest position of all: Prime Minister.

H.M. THE KING.

Camera Portrait by

Far left *The German Emperor William II, under whose leadership Germany grew to be a major world power in the early years of this century.*

Left *King George V of England, grandson of Queen Victoria and cousin of William II. The rivalry between the cousins was a personal aspect of the competition between Britain and Germany.*

Prime Minister

Above *British people queuing for food after the introduction of rationing in 1917.*

Lloyd George said that when he became Prime Minister he felt he was 'the most miserable man on earth'. If this was so, he certainly did not show it. Within weeks he had reorganized the government and given the country the inspired new leadership it was looking for.

Operating with a small, all-party War Cabinet, the Prime Minister made rapid and important decisions. He forced the navy to adopt the successful convoy system to protect merchant ships bringing important supplies from abroad. In 1918, he introduced limited food rationing to ensure that items were fairly distributed.

The Prime Minister had little faith in the generals responsible for managing the war in France. At times he misled them and made secret plans, as when he arranged for the British army to be placed under the French Commander, General Nivelle, in 1917. Nevertheless, Lloyd George's brilliant oratory ensured that he always had the support of the House of Commons, whatever tricks his critics might accuse him of.

During the war, and while he was negotiating the terms of the peace treaty that followed, Lloyd George was backed by the Conservative Party; but by 1922, Conservative support for a Liberal Prime Minister was weakening. Finally, in October of that year the Conservatives decided to fight the next general election alone. Lloyd George's six years of power were over.

Right *Lloyd George's War Cabinet. The members (from left to right) are: Arthur Henderson (Labour), Andrew Bonar Law (Conservative), Winston Churchill (Liberal), Lord Milner (non-party), Lloyd George (Liberal), Lord Curzon (Conservative), Maurice Hankey (Cabinet Secretary).*

The wilderness years

Lloyd George was a politician of genius. In his day he was the best speaker in the House of Commons, and he was inspired by a strong sense of justice for the oppressed. His quick and penetrating mind was tempered by charm and a fine sense of humour.

Nevertheless, Lloyd George made many enemies. Several Liberals felt that the way he had replaced Henry Asquith in 1916 was disgraceful: they remained loyal to their old leader, and caused a split in the Liberal Party. The Conservatives did not trust Lloyd George's devious ways. In 1912, for example, he had made a great deal of money out of a shady stock exchange deal. His name was only cleared after a long official enquiry. Furthermore, Lloyd George's many love affairs meant that his personal life was a constant source of scandal.

As a result, after 1922 Lloyd George was never again called upon to serve his country. He could still captivate the House of Commons with his speeches, but he spent much of his time writing books such as his *War Memoirs* and *The Truth about the Peace Treaties*. However, when he died in 1945, Winston Churchill accurately recalled before the House of Commons that in the first quarter of the twentieth century, 'The greater part of our fortunes, in peace and war, were shaped by this one man: David Lloyd George'.

Right *Although he never again held political office after 1922, Lloyd George remained a brilliant speaker whose words were always listened to with respect by other MPs.*

The armed camps

In the early twentieth century, the major European powers were ranged against each other in two armed camps, each bound together by a web of agreements and alliances. Since the most powerful countries had world empires, there was hardly a major nation, except the United States, that was not in some way concerned with the European balance of power.

The oldest alliance was that between the German and the Austro-Hungarian Empires, forming a power bloc that dominated central Europe – called the Central Powers. Italy and the new state of Bulgaria were allied to the Central Powers, who were also on good terms with the vast Turkish Empire.

Since a war of 1870–71, France had been bitterly opposed to Germany. She had strengthened her position in 1893–94 by forming an alliance with Russia. The Russians cast greedy eyes on the Balkan countries, regarding themselves as protectors of the Slav peoples who lived there. For a long while Britain remained aloof from the European network of alliances until, in 1904, she made a friendly agreement with France called the Entente Cordiale. This was followed in 1907 by a similar agreement with Russia.

By 1910, therefore, with two armed camps ranged against each other, the European political situation was very dangerous. Any badly-handled crisis might lead to war.

Above *Tsar Nicholas II of Russia was related by marriage to the British royal family. He was determined to support the tiny state of Serbia against her mighty neighbour, the Austro-Hungarian Empire.*

Left *Long before war broke out in 1914, there had been tension along the frontiers of Europe. Nations were in a state of constant readiness in case their enemies tried to launch a surprise attack.*

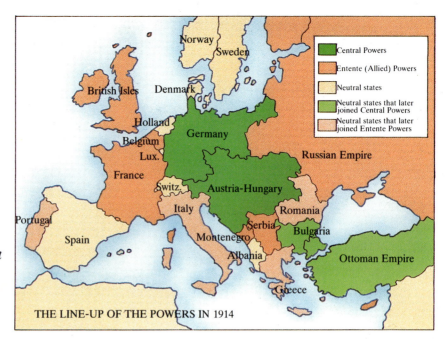

THE LINE-UP OF THE POWERS IN 1914

Legend:
- Central Powers
- Entente (Allied) Powers
- Neutral states
- Neutral states that later joined Central Powers
- Neutral states that later joined Entente Powers

This map suggests how well-balanced the two sides in the First World War were. Only when the United States joined the Allies in 1917 was the balance tipped decidedly in their favour.

Sarajevo

On several occasions the two European power blocs came close to armed conflict. In 1905 and 1911 the two were in dispute over Morocco. Tension was particularly high between France and Germany. On each occasion Germany backed down, humiliated.

The situation in the Balkans was even more dangerous. The once-mighty Muslim Turkish Empire was in decline and the peoples that had been subject to the Empire's rule struggled for independence. Greece led the way in 1829, followed later by Romania, Serbia, Bulgaria and other smaller states. By 1914 the Balkans were dotted with proud, newly-independent nations, each suspicious of its neighbour, and all afraid of being swallowed up by the super-powers adjoining the region.

In 1909 Austria–Hungary had annexed the Balkan states of Bosnia and Herzegovina. This act was resented by Russia, who regarded herself as protector of the Balkan slavic nations, and particularly of Serbia. Relations between Serbia and Austria–Hungary grew worse.

On 28 June, 1914 the heir to the Austrian throne, Archduke Francis Ferdinand and his wife were assassinated in Sarajevo, the capital of Bosnia. Austria accused the Serbs of organizing the killings. 'We feel confident,' observed Lloyd George, 'that . . . common sense . . . will enable us to pull through these difficulties.' How wrong he was proved to be.

Below *The Archduke Franz Ferdinand, heir to the throne of the Austro-Hungarian Empire, was assassinated by the terrorist, Gabriel Princip in June 1914. Many people feared an international crisis might follow but no-one expected a world war.*

World War

During the month which followed the Sarajevo assassination, Europe buzzed with diplomatic activity. Finally, on 27 July, Austria–Hungary acted, sending an ultimatum containing a list of impossible demands to the Serbs. Serbia had to accept this ultimatum or face war with its giant neighbour. Assured of Russian support, Serbia rejected the ultimatum and on 28 July, Austria–Hungary invaded.

Russia, Serbia's ally, started to mobilize forces. Seeking to strike first, on 1 August Germany declared war on Russia and two days later launched an attack on Russia's ally, France, advancing through the neutral country of Belgium. The entry into Belgium was in

British troops going 'over the top' in an attack. Men were often so exhausted after crossing no–man's–land with heavy packs and equipment that they had no strength left to fight.

direct breach of the neutrality that Germany itself had previously guaranteed.

For some years Britain's relations with Germany had been deteriorating. The Germans had tried to aid Britain's enemies in the Anglo-Boer War of 1899–1902. There was also commercial, colonial and naval rivalry between the two empires. Nevertheless, before the invasion of Belgium, there was no direct reason for Britain to get involved in the conflict. Lloyd George and several of his cabinet colleagues felt this strongly.

However, Britain had guaranteed Belgian neutrality in 1839, so an ultimatum was sent to Germany, demanding that German forces leave Belgium. Germany refused, and on 4 August Britain declared war on Germany. Before long the fighting spread from Europe to Africa, the Far East and the oceans: a European squabble had become world war.

Above The End of a Dog Fight *by A. Boult, 1917. Aeroplanes did not play a major part in the First World War because their range was short and they could not carry heavy loads.*

3 THE WESTERN FRONT

A war of attrition

In 1905 General Count von Schlieffen, Chief of the General Staff, had presented a plan to his leader, the German Kaiser, which would enable Germany to fight both Russia and France at the same time. He envisaged a rapid and unexpected German strike on France through neutral Belgium. With Paris captured, he calculated that France would surrender and that Britain would come to terms, releasing all the German forces to oppose Russia. The plan failed.

By the Christmas of 1914 Allied forces had halted the German attack and both sides had dug in.

Below *The machine gun dominated much of the fighting in the First World War. Here we see gunners wearing protective clothing in case of an attack by poisonous gas.*

Two lines of trenches snaked across Europe from the Channel to Switzerland. Defended by barbed wire and machine guns, these lines proved almost impossible to penetrate. Most of the horrific fighting on the Western Front consisted of vain attempts to achieve a breakthrough.

In 1915 the fighting was particularly fierce around the town of Ypres, where poisoned gas was used for the first time. The next year, while the Germans sought to 'bleed France white' at Verdun, the British counter-attacked near the River Somme, losing 66,000 men on the first day. By 1917 the French were incapable of further offensives, while the British continued to struggle with increasing helplessness. 'We are losing the flower of our army, and to what purpose?' Lloyd-George asked angrily. Only in 1918, with American help for the Allies arriving in increasing strength did the stalemate end. By then millions had perished.

Above Gassed and Wounded *by E. Kennington. Poisonous gas was used by both sides in the war. It inflicted terrible burns and left many men blinded.*

Life in the trenches

Trench warfare was described as a living hell for soldiers on both sides. The exhausted men lived in damp, rat-infested conditions, waiting for the next assault.

In his memoirs Lloyd George described the fighting in the trenches on the Western Front as 'one of the horrors of history'. For months and even years, men lived in damp, dirty dugouts. They were shot at, shelled and gassed. Their bodies crawled with lice, their feet rotted in wet boots. And still they were ordered to climb out of the trenches and charge the barbed wire and machine guns of the enemy.

The zig-zag trenches were usually three deep, with communication trenches connecting them. Between the two front lines lay no-man's-land, often strewn with shattered trees and barbed wire on which the

bodies of the dead still hung. After an attack the cries of the wounded in no-man's-land haunted the living, who could do little to help their dying comrades.

The men lived in holes carved into the trench sides. In many parts of the German lines these were deep and strongly made with concrete, but the British and French were less well-sheltered. Drinking water came up to the front line in cans and was often dirty and in short supply. The food was of poor quality.

In these terrible conditions epidemics swept through the armies. Thousands died of diseases such as cholera, dysentry or gangrene. It is small wonder that men sometimes deliberately tried to get wounded, so that they could be sent home. They even inflicted wounds upon themselves, risking court martial and the death penalty.

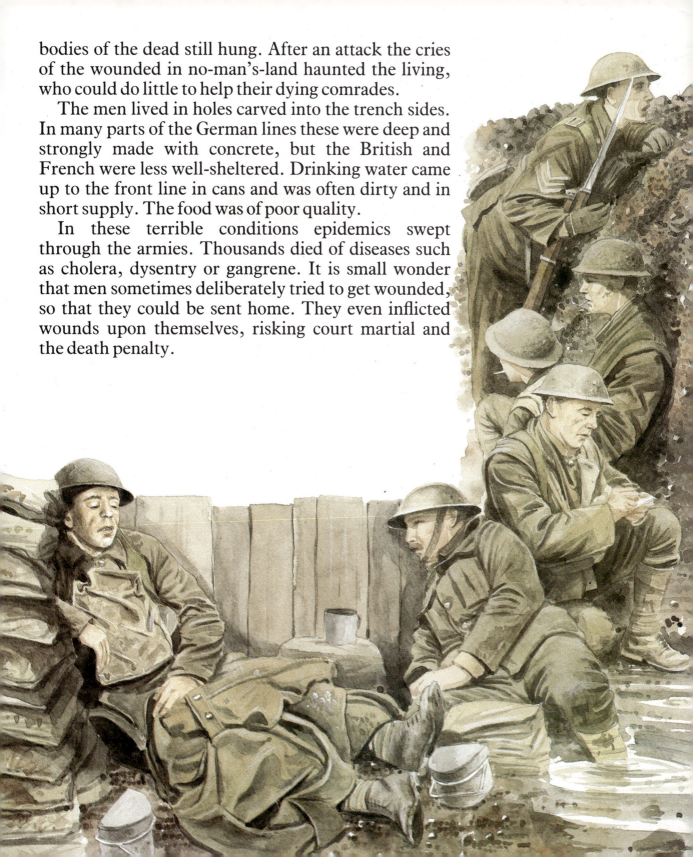

Turning points

In the end nobody won the fighting on the Western Front. At the cease-fire at 11 am on 11 November 1918, the German armies had retreated many miles but they were not defeated. In fact, on two occasions during the fighting the German armies came very close to a breakthrough.

By early September 1914, some German troops were within sight of Paris. The French and British forces made their stand on the River Marne to the east of Paris. Every available soldier was brought from Paris by bus and taxi, and at a crucial stage in the battle a spotter plane noticed a gap in the German line.

Below *German troops within sight of Paris. Twice, in 1914 and 1918, they nearly reached the city but each time they were turned back by determined allied resistance.*

The British advanced slowly, the Germans fell back, and Paris was saved. The German General von Kluck ruefully told the Kaiser, 'We have lost the war.'

The Germans also came very close to breakthrough in 1918, when General Ludendorff launched a final great offensive. They were able to concentrate their forces on the Western Front after the Russian collapse in 1917 had removed pressure from the Eastern Front. All along the front, highly-trained stormtroopers found the weak points in the Allied line and broke through. Once more Paris came within German artillery range but, as in 1914, the Allies grimly hung on. By May the Germans were exhausted and demoralized as more and more American troops joined the Allies. Ludendorff's bid for victory had failed.

Above *The German General Erich Ludendorff (1865–1937) played a major part in the shattering defeat of the Russians in 1914 and almost succeeded in breaking the Allied lines in spring, 1918.*

4 EASTERN EUROPE

The Eastern Front

The enormous resources of the Russian Empire enabled it to put two million soldiers in the field in 1914, and by 1916 Russian armies totalled fifteen million men. These forces were thought of as a steamroller: slow but unstoppable.

However, the Russian armies were stopped. In 1914 the Germans inflicted two heavy defeats on them at Tannenberg and the Masurian lakes, in East Prussia. The next year the Russians were driven further back and despite a brave offensive under General Brusilov in 1916, the armies collapsed and Russia was overtaken by revolutions which began in March 1917. In November the Communists under Lenin seized power and made peace with the Germans. At the humiliating treaty of Brest–Litovsk (March 1918) Russia had to surrender 33 per cent of her population and 40 per cent of her industry to Germany.

The armies of the Austro–Hungarian Empire were involved in campaigns on two fronts, apart from that with Russia. They did not crush Serbia as swiftly as had been anticipated; the conquest was not complete until 1916.

Italy was promised extensive territory to the north by the Allies, and so joined them in 1915. For two years there was stalemate in the Alps until the Austrians broke through at Caporetto, forcing the allies rapidly to reinforce the Italian armies. These reorganized forces finally defeated the Austrians at Vittoria Veneto, and Austria–Hungary sued for peace a short time later.

Above *The Russian Communist leader Vladimir Lenin (1870–1924) addressing a meeting of workers and revolutionaries. One of the first things he did after seizing power in November 1917 was to make peace with the Germans.*

Far left *Italian troops fighting in the Alps. Although the terrain was different along this front, for much of the war there was the same stalemate as in the west.*

The soft underbelly

By the end of 1914, with the Germans advancing into Russia and no progress being made on the Western Front, soldiers and politicians sought a new strategy to break the deadlock. Winston Churchill, First Lord of the Admiralty, put forward a plan to attack the Dardanelles, the narrow entrance to the Black Sea, so diverting the forces of the Central Powers away from the Western and Eastern Fronts. Churchill described the proposed area of assault as the 'soft underbelly' of Europe.

At first British and French warships tried bombarding Turkish positions, but they suffered very heavy casualties from mines and gunfire, so landings were made on the Gallipoli peninsula which overlooked the approach to the Dardanelles.

Below *Allied troops landing at Gallipoli in an attempt to divert the attention of the Central Powers away from Russia.*

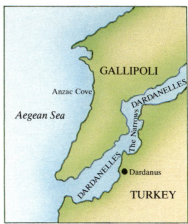

British, Australian and New Zealand troops were put ashore with little preparation and no orders. They were soon pinned down by fierce Turkish resistance. More landings followed in August, but they too failed. During the hot Mediterranean summer thousands of Allied troops died in the insanitary trenches. Finally, in December 1915 and January 1916, the survivors were evacuated and the disastrous campaign brought to an end.

A second Allied landing in southern Europe, at Salonika in October 1915, was somewhat more successful. Lloyd George strongly supported this scheme to break what he called the 'eternal stalemate on the other lines'. Although they failed to save Serbia, troops from Salonika eventually defeated Bulgaria and made inroads into both the Austro–Hungarian and Turkish Empires.

5 WAR ELSEWHERE

The Middle East

In August 1914 two mighty German warships, the *Goeben* and the *Breslau*, were chased into Constantinople harbour by the British Mediterranean fleet. Before the war Turkey had been on good terms with Austria–Hungary and Germany, but had not immediately declared war to support them. However, when the German ships turned their guns on Constantinople, the Turkish capital city, the Turks had little option but to join the war on the side of Germany and Austria–Hungary.

As the Turkish Empire stretched right across the Middle East, the Turks found themselves fighting in several areas at once: in the Balkans, at Gallipoli and in the north against Russia. They were also fighting in Mesopotamia (modern-day Iraq) and Palestine, where the British were defending lines of communication with India. An Anglo–Indian force attacked into what is modern Iraq in defence of the oil-fields of the Persian Gulf. In 1916 the first army was destroyed at Kut but in 1918 a second, larger force seized Baghdad.

To the west, General Allenby led a British army from Cairo, across the Suez Canal, towards Palestine. Meanwhile the Arabs under Turkish rule in Arabia had risen in revolt. In the eccentric Englishman T.E. Lawrence, they found a leader of considerable skill, who enabled them to join with Allenby by October 1918 and take Damascus, the key city of the region.

Above *Colonel T.E. Lawrence (1888–1935) played a major part in the Arab defeat of the Turks in Arabia.*

Left *After long years of fighting, the Arab forces from Arabia and Jordan joined with those of General Allenby to occupy Damascus in 1918. Here, British troops enter the key city of the eastern Mediterranean.*

Africa and the Far East

In 1902 Britain had made a military treaty with Japan, the new formidable Far-Eastern power. When war broke out this alliance proved very useful because the Japanese were able to join with British imperial forces to assault the German colonies and trading ports in the region. Moreover, the Japanese navy commanded the eastern Pacific, freeing British ships for duty elsewhere.

The African continent had been carved up by the imperial powers in the second half of the nineteenth century. Although the British took a larger share of the continent than anyone else, the Germans had several colonies, particularly in the south. Therefore, after

Above *Japanese troops captured several German possessions in the Far East. Here they are cutting through barbed wire to attack a German colony in China.*

war had broken out in Europe it was not long before it spread to Africa.

Three German colonies were overcome quite rapidly. An Anglo–Nigerian army took the Cameroons (now a republic in West Africa). Togoland (now part of Ghana and Togo) was occupied by British and French soldiers, while troops from South Africa invaded German South-West Africa (now Namibia). However in German East Africa (Tanzania) the story was rather different.

General von Lettow-Vorbeck masterminded a brilliant German defence. With a mere 5,000 men he resisted 130,000 allies, only surrendering when he heard of the armistice in Europe. The campaign to take German East Africa was expensive costing the allies £72 million.

Below *Allied troops marching in Africa. All but one of Germany's African colonies were soon overcome by Allied forces.*

6   THE WAR AT SEA

Jutland

The First World War was not won on land but at sea. By late 1918 Germany faced starvation owing to an effective allied naval blockade of German ports. This blockade worked only because Britain was able to maintain control of the waters of the Atlantic.

When Germany started a naval building programme in the late nineteenth century, Britain regarded the new fleet as 'an expensive luxury' which deliberately challenged traditional British naval superiority. Britain responded by building a new type of powerful

Although the British lost more men and ships at the great naval Battle of Jutland (1916), the German fleet never put to sea again. Both sides claimed victory.

battleship, the Dreadnought, thus fuelling a naval arms race.

For the first two years of the war there was little important naval action between surface vessels. Then, on 31 May, 1916 the German High Seas Fleet, which had been in port all the war, put to sea. From its Scottish bases the British navy steamed to intercept. Admiral Beatty's battlecruiser squadron was first to reach the Germans and suffered serious losses. Then the main British fleet arrived, commanded by Admiral Jellicoe, and the Germans skilfully turned for home in the gathering dusk.

Although fighting continued through the night the Germans managed to return safely to base at Wilhelmshaven. They had lost fewer ships and far fewer men than the British, but they never again put to sea. The blockade of Germany stood firm.

The U-boat

Britain was and still is a trading and manufacturing nation which depends heavily upon imports of food and materials from all corners of the world. When war broke out in 1914 the Germans were quick to see how vulnerable Britain was. They decided to impose a blockade using a new type of ship – the submarine.

At first the German unterseeboot (U-boat) fleet attacked only Allied vessels, and Britain was kept supplied by ships from neutral countries, such as the United States. Then, in February 1915, the Germans

declared war zones around Britain in which they would sink all vessels. This plan was very unpopular with neutral countries and for a while, after the torpedoing of the liner *Lusitania* with the loss of 1,153 lives, the Germans relaxed their grip.

However, the next year the U-boats returned to a policy of unrestricted sinking. By early 1917 the situation in Britain was desperate, with only six weeks' supply of food remaining. Lloyd George, the new Prime Minister, finally persuaded the navy to try the convoy system. This meant that merchant vessels sailed in close formation, protected by warships. The convoys managed to get through the blockade and it collapsed. By 1918, as the allied navies developed more effective anti-submarine weapons, such as depth charges, the war against the U-boat had been won. But for Britain it had been a very close thing indeed.

The sinking of the ship Lusitania *in May, 1915. 1,153 people were killed when the great liner was torpedoed by a German U-boat without warning. The incident helped to turn the United States against Germany, since 128 Americans were among the dead.*

7 ALLIED VICTORY

The Home Front

Are **YOU** in this?

Above *War posters encouraged everyone to contribute to the war effort.*

Below *Women in Britain ably taking over the jobs of men fighting at the front.*

The First World War was the first large-scale total war. Almost everyone living in the warring countries was involved in the war effort, as the whole of a nation's industrial, agricultural, military and political resources were geared to winning the war. In Britain, Lloyd George was more responsible than anyone else for organizing the country for war.

British people talked of the 'home front'. They were bombed by German airships called Zeppelins and were short of food. But conscription, compulsory military service, was the aspect of the war which affected them most. Conscription was common in most European countries before 1914. It was first introduced in Britain in 1916, to Lloyd George's bitter disappointment. As a result there was hardly a family in Europe that did

Left *Britain was bombed by German airships, called Zeppelins after their inventor Count Ferdinand von Zeppelin. The airships had a cigar-shaped aluminium frame covered in cotton cloth and could attain speeds of up to 32 km/h.*

not suffer bereavement.

With a large proportion of the male work force at the front, women took over much of their work in the factories and on the farms. This helped the cause of women's rights, as it showed that they could do what had previously been considered men's work. In 1918 many British women were given the right to vote in Parliamentary elections.

It was the civilian population in Germany who finally ended the war, tired of the deprivation and slaughter. On 9 November, 1918 there was a general strike in Berlin. Soldiers and sailors mutinied, the Kaiser fled abroad, and the government asked the Allied forces for an armistice.

Enter America

In 1914 the United States of America had no quarrel with either side in a war which they saw as a European squabble. Therefore, despite strong links of friendship with Britain, the United States remained neutral.

When German submarine attacks on neutral shipping began in February 1915 American opinion started to change. In May, 128 Americans died when the *Lusitania* was sunk off Ireland. In 1916 more and more American ships were sunk, but still President Wilson could not move without the consent of Congress. 'He is awaiting another insult before he actually draws the sword!' complained Lloyd George.

Finally, in 1917 British intelligence intercepted a secret telegram from Germany to Mexico, promising Texas to the Mexicans if they would join the war on the side of the Central Powers. Six more American ships were sunk, and the United States declared war on Germany on 6 April, 1917.

The entry of the United States into the war greatly boosted the Allies' morale. Although it was many months before its effect was felt – the first American troops landed in France in July 1917 – the might of the United States enabled the tide to be turned on the Western Front, and American naval and merchant ships helped in the battle against the U-boat. Without American intervention, the war might have dragged on for years longer.

Right *American soldiers about to embark for Europe. The arrival of these troops turned the war decisively in the Allies favour.*

8 PEACE

Versailles

Producing a peace settlement after the First World War proved almost as difficult as winning the war itself. With the disintegration of the German, Austro–Hungarian, Russian and Turkish Empires, the political map of Europe had changed beyond recognition. Moreover, the victors had different aims: President Wilson of the USA sought to build a new and fairer world from the ruins of the old, while Britain and particularly France were more concerned with gaining revenge.

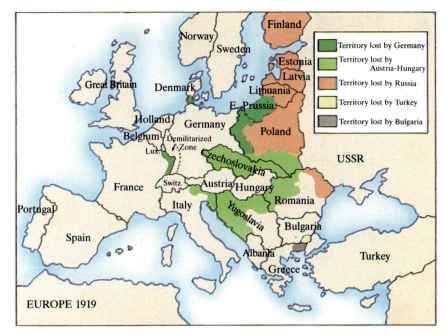

Territory lost by Germany
Territory lost by Austria-Hungary
Territory lost by Russia
Territory lost by Turkey
Territory lost by Bulgaria

EUROPE 1919

This map shows how Europe had been altered by the War. If you compare it with the map on page 14 you will see how much territory Germany had to surrender to the Allies.

The Germans were not invited to Versailles, the palace outside Paris where the negotiations which decided their fate were held. Orlando, the Italian Prime Minister, was so dissatisfied with the talks that he walked out. Separate discussions decided the fates of Austria, Hungary, Turkey and Bulgaria.

The Treaty of Versailles was signed on 28 June, 1919. By its terms Germany lost all her colonies and a great deal of territory: Alsace–Lorraine, for example, was returned to France. Germany was permitted to keep only a tiny army of 100,000 men, a navy of ships of less than 10,000 tons, with no submarines, and no airforce. The Germans also had to accept that they had caused the war and, therefore, pay the victors £6,000 million in compensation. Lloyd George, a prominent figure at Versailles, was not happy with the terms: 'We shall have to do the whole thing over again in twenty-five years,' he predicted, 'at three times the cost.'

Left *The 'Big Four' at the Versailles Peace Conference: from left to right Orlando, Prime Minister of Italy; Lloyd George; Clemenceau, Prime Minister of France; Woodrow Wilson, President of the United States.*

All in vain?

The Treaties signed after the First World War established The League of Nations, an organization designed to promote international peace and co-operation. It sought to mediate in disputes between nations and to take the lead in humanitarian matters, such as helping refugees. However, several of the major states, among whom were the United States and Russia, did not join the League, which also had no power to enforce its decisions.

The war had ruined the economies of most European countries. Throughout the Continent there was high unemployment, civil violence and serious instability. In Russia, following the revolutions of 1917, the Communists had seized power, while Italy came under the control of a Fascist dictator, Benito Mussolini in 1922. In Germany, however, the new democratic system of government survived, and by the late 1920s the country was beginning to get back on its feet again.

Then in 1929 a major world wide economic recession began, plunging Germany once more into deprivation and unemployment. Skilfully using the depressed state of their country, the Nazis under Adolph Hitler gained control. Hitler, who had fought in the trenches of the Western Front, promised the Germans that he would erase the shame of Versailles and make them a great nation again. Before long it seemed as if the appalling slaughter of the First World War had been in vain.

Above *The harsh conditions imposed by the Treaty of Versailles paved the way for the rise of the Nazis in the 1930s. It was not long before the humiliated German people turned to Adolf Hitler to restore their shattered country.*

Left *A ceasefire was called on the Western Front at 11 am on 11 November, 1918. Poppies, which flowered in the battlefields of France have been looked upon as symbols of the tragic slaughter and waste of human life ever since.*

43

Table of dates

1863	Lloyd George born.
1871	German Empire formed.
1879	Dual Alliance between Germany and Austria.
1890	Lloyd George enters Parliament as MP for Caernarvon Boroughs.
1894	Franco–Russian alliance.
1898	German government passes Navy Law for the building of more battleships.
1902	Anglo–Japanese alliance.
1904	Anglo–French entente.
1905–6	Franco–German tension over Morocco.
1906	Lloyd George President of the Board of Trade. *HMS Dreadnought* launched.
1907	Anglo–Russian entente.
1908	Lloyd George Chancellor of the Exchequer.
1911	Second Moroccan crisis.
1914	28 June Archduke Francis Ferdinand of Austro–Hungary and his wife assassinated at Sarajevo in Bosnia. 28 July Austro–Hungary declares war on Serbia. 1 August Germany declares war on Russia. 3 August Germany declares war on France and invades Belgium. 4 August Britain declares war on Germany. 27 August Russians defeated at Battle of Tannenburg.
	5–11 September German advance in the west held at the Battle of the Marne.
1915	19 February Dardanelles campaign begins. 22 April second Battle of Ypres begins. 7 May *SS Lusitania* sunk by a German submarine. 24 May Italy declares war on Austria–Hungary. 28 May Lloyd George Minister of Munitions.
1916	21 February German attack on Verdun begins. 31 May Battle of Jutland. 5 June Russian offensive under General Brusilov begins. 1 July British attack on the Somme begins. 6 December Lloyd George becomes Prime Minister.
1917	8 March Revolution in Russia. 6 April USA declares war on Germany. 24 October Italians defeated at Caporetto. 4 November Passchendaele captured by Allies. 6–7 November Communists seize power in Russia.
1918	3 March Russians accept peace at Brest–Litovsk. 21 March Ludendorff launches final German offensive. 18 July Ludendorff offensive held at Battle of Marne. 9 November Kaiser abdicates. 11 November Armistice was signed.
1919	Treaty of Versailles signed.

1921	Lloyd George seems to solve the Irish problem by setting up the Irish Free State (Eire).	1933	Hitler comes to power in Germany.
1922	Lloyd George resigns as Prime Minister.	1939	Outbreak of the Second World War.
		1945	Death of Lloyd George.

Glossary

Alliance A partnership formed by two or more countries by treaty for military purposes.

Armistice An agreement to stop fighting.

Assassination A political murder.

Attrition A gradual wearing down. A war of attrition is one whose outcome depends on which side can last longer.

Balkans The countries of the Balkan peninsula: Yugoslavia, Romania, Bulgaria, Albania, Greece and the European part of Turkey.

Budget A country's financial plans.

Cabinet The chief ministers of the government.

Campaign A long-term battle plan.

Chancellor of the Exchequer The Minister responsible for Britain's economy.

Colony Land in possession of an overseas power.

Compensation The payment of money to make amends for damage.

Depth charges Bombs that explode in the water at pre-set depths.

Dictator A person in sole charge of a non-democratic country.

Economy All a country's resources.

Empire Lands of different parts of the world ruled by one powerful country.

Epidemic A widespread outbreak of a disease.

Evacuate To remove or clear out.

Fascist Authoritarian, racist and anti-communist.

Mine A bomb on land or sea which explodes when touched.

Mobilize To prepare for war, to call up the armed forces for active service.

Munitions Weapons and ammunition.

Mutiny Refusal to obey commands in the armed forces.

Neutrality The state of not taking sides in a dispute or contest.

Offensive Large-scale attack.

Oratory The art of public-speaking.

Radical One who seeks fundamental (basic) change.

Rationing The limitation of what is available to make it last.

Recession Economic decline.

Stock exchange The place where investments are bought and sold.

Strategy Planning the course of war campaigns.

Torpedo An underwater missile.

Treaty An official agreement.

Ultimatum A final statement of terms, under threat of war.

Zeppelins Large German air ships.

Further information

Books

A Family in World War I, A. Vincent. How They Lived series (Wayland, 1987).

Britain at War, 1914–1919, C. Mair (Murray, 1982).

Growing up in the First World War, P. Warner (Wayland, 1980).

Lloyd George, P. Rowland (Barrie and Jenkins, 1975). This is a huge book, written for adults, but it contains all you could wish to know about Lloyd George.

Spotlight on the First World War, Michael Gibson. The Spotlight on History series (Wayland, 1985).

The First World War, A.J.P. Taylor (Penguin, 1966).

The Great War, R. Tames (Batsford, 1984).

The Origins of World War I, R. Parkinson (Wayland, 1972).

Tommy Goes to War, M. Brown (Dent, 1980).

Places to visit

Museums

There are many museums in the Allied countries open to the public, which have displays or exhibits relating to World War I. It is worth investigating your local museums for information. Well worth a visit in Britain are the Imperial War Museum, London SE7; the National Army Museum, Chelsea SW3 and the National Maritime Museum, Greenwich.

Famous sites

If you have a chance, visit the battlefields of Flanders in France, a fascinating and moving experience.

Libraries

Your local library will have plenty of biographies of Lloyd George and books on World War I. See if you can find any of the books mentioned in the reading list.

Picture acknowledgements

E.T. Archives 17, 19; Mary Evans Picture Library 23, 25, 27, 29, 30; The Mansell Collection 5, 7 (both), 13, 37, 43; Malcolm S. Walker 14, 27 (map), 41; Wayland Picture Library 8, 36.

Index